Fabulous
Friendship Bracelets

This edition published in 2013
By SpiceBox™
12171 Horseshoe Way,
Richmond, BC,
Canada V7A 4V4

First published in 2007
Text and artwork copyright © 2007

ISBN 10: 1-894722-49-3
ISBN 13: 978-1-894722-49-0

CEO and Publisher: Ben Lotfi
Editorial: Trisha Pope
Creative Director: Garett Chan
Art Director: Christine Covert
Design & Layout: Morgen Matheson and Charmaine Muzyka
Production: James Badger and Mell D'Clute
Sourcing: Janny Lam
Photography: Garett Chan and James Badger

For more SpiceBox products and information, visit our website:
www.spicebox.ca

Manufactured in China

13 15 17 19 20 18 16 14

Special thanks to the models: Cristina Soares, Renee Lawless, Jorgina
Thompson, Jamie Lacamell, Kelly Chan, and Claudia Chan

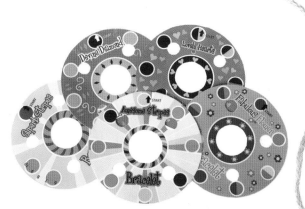

Let's Make Bracelets!

by the Spicebox Fun Team

Table of Contents

Introduction

Friendship bracelets are a fun and simple craft to make, and this book and kit provide you with everything you will need to make dozens of these pretty accessories; plenty of colorful thread and step-by-step instructions, as well as a really neat Friendship Wheel tool to help you create more complicated woven bracelets. Why not invite some of your friends over, and have a bracelet-making party? You can exchange them with each other, and then every time you look at the one tied on your wrist you will remember the stories and fun times you shared with your friends while you made them.

Friendship bracelets have a charming tradition to them that you should pass on when you give them away. Help fasten the bracelet onto your friend's wrist and tell them to make a wish. When the bracelet is worn out and comes off their wrist, the wish will come true. But if they take it off themselves, the wish will may come true, so be careful!

Did you know: that once you accept a friendship bracelet from someone, you must wear it until it naturally wears out and falls off. If you take it off sooner than this, it means that you no longer want to be friends with the person who gave it to you!

Interesting Fact:
The origin of friendship bracelets is most likely Central American countries where they are a traditional handicraft. They only became popular in North America in the 1970s, but have remained popular ever since.

Look at your pattern template and select the strings to match the colors on the tabs. For each color tab, you will need one string in that color. Cut your strings 20 inches/ 50 cm long. Leave about 2 inches/ 5 cm at the end and then tie the strings into a knot.

OR

For every pair of same-colored tabs on the wheel, cut 1 string 40 inches/100 cm long. To create a loop at the end of your bracelet, fold the strings in half over a pencil and then tie the strings into a knot, pulling the knot tight up to the pencil. You should now have as many strings as the pattern requires in the correct colors.

Setting Up the Friendship Bracelet Wheel.

Setting up the wheel properly is the first step to using the friendship wheel. Regardless of the pattern you choose, you will need to set up the wheel the same way. Follow these steps carefully to get started.

1. Prepare your strings according to the chart below, referring to the instructions on pages 11 and 12 for help, if you need it.

2. Set your wheel on the table with the "START" arrow positioned at 12 o'clock (at the top of the wheel).

3. Place your strings so that the knot is in the hole in the middle of the wheel, and the strings are fanned out so that you can pick them up easily.

4. Hold the knot down in the center of the wheel with one finger so that it doesn't move, and with your other hand, pick up a string and notch it into the wheel of a tab of the same color.

5. Continue to hold the knot in place while you position all of the strings into tabs of the matching color. Once they are all in place pick up the wheel and adjust any strings that are loose. Your wheel is now set up and you can start making the bracelets!

video tutorial

	40 in/100cm	20 in/50cm
Yellow	2	4
Blue	2	4
Purple	2	4
Red or Green	2	4

13

Let's make the Awesome Stripes Bracelet.

	40 in/100cm	20 in/50cm
Yellow	2	4
Blue	2	4
Purple	2	4
Red or Green	2	4

1. Prepare your threads according to the chart.

2. Set up your wheel following the instructions on page 13.

3. Position your wheel so that the Start arrow is at the top.

4. There should be two yellow strings in the two notches at the top of your wheel and two at the bottom. Unhook the TOP RIGHT string from the wheel.

5. Move the string to the bottom of the wheel, and hook it into the tab beside the BOTTOM RIGHT string.

6. Unhook the BOTTOM LEFT string and rehook it into the notch to the left of the TOP LEFT string. Check to make sure your wheel now looks like the diagram:

7. Turn your wheel counterclockwise, or to the LEFT one tab. The BLUE strings should now be at the top of your wheel.

8. Unhook the TOP RIGHT blue string and hook it back into the wheel beside the BOTTOM RIGHT string.

9. Unhook the BOTTOM LEFT string and rehook it to the left of the TOP LEFT string.

10. Turn the wheel to the left - counter clockwise - until the green strings are at the top. Continue hooking and rehooking your strings in this way, and you will see your bracelet grow! Remember: At the top, unhook from the right, and rehook to the right. At the bottom, unhook from the left, and rehook to the left.

To Finish: When your bracelet is long enough, unhook all the strings, being careful not to tangle them up. Tie them in a knot at the bottom, and trim the bracelet neatly, making sure you have enough thread to tie it onto your wrist.

2

4

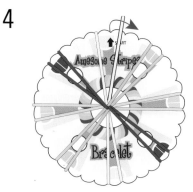

5

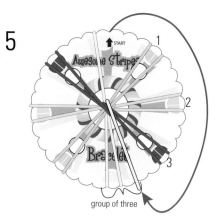

group of three

6

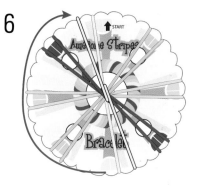

7

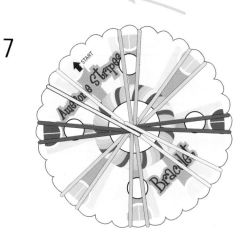

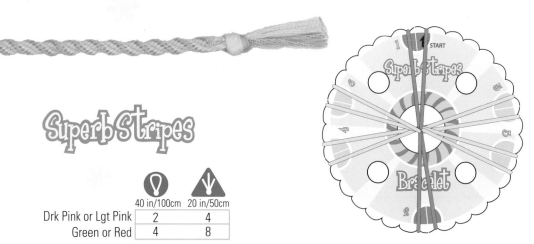

Superb Stripes

	⬤ 40 in/100cm	▽ 20 in/50cm
Drk Pink or Lgt Pink	2	4
Green or Red	4	8

This pattern is a bit different because there are fewer strings and tabs and you are also not going to spin your wheel as you knot. Start your bracelet in the same way, by cutting and knotting your strings and then stringing them onto the wheel in the correct notches. Then, follow these instructions:

1. Unhook the TAB1 right string and move it to the right notch of TAB2
2. Unhook the left string of TAB2 and rehook it to the left of TAB1
3. Unhook the TAB3 right string and move it to the right notch of TAB4
4. Unhook the left string of TAB4 and rehook it to the left of TAB3
5. Unhook the TAB5 right string and move it to the right notch of TAB6
6. Unhook the left string of TAB6 and rehook it to the left of TAB5
7. Move each string CLOCKWISE (to the RIGHT) so that they are lined up on the tabs again.

Repeat steps 1-7 until your bracelet is long enough to tie on.

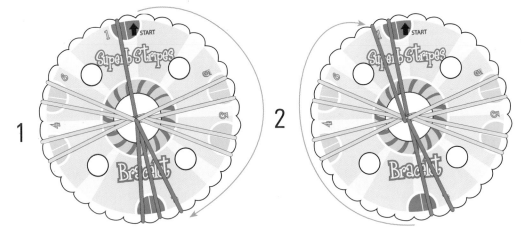

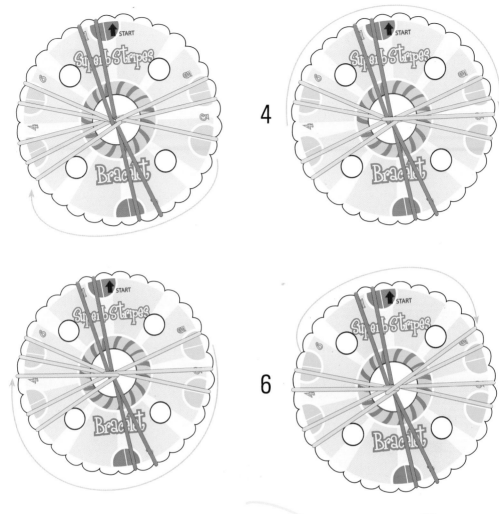

3

4

5

6

7

19

Traditional Style

Flat Friendship Bracelet styles

Variation: Cut three threads that are long enough to wrap around your waist two times. Using the same techniques, create a skinny belt for your waist that you can wear with shorts or jeans. Super stylish! You can also make it with more than three threads for a thicker twist.

A Right-loop Knot

1. Knot two pieces of thread and tape them to a board. Hold the second string (2) firmly and cross the first string (1) over it, leaving a round loop made of the second string (2).

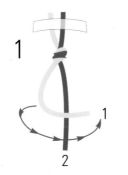

2. Send the first string (1) under the second string (2) and up through the loop. Softly pull on it to make a knot. Slide the knot up to the top of the board, and pull it tight.

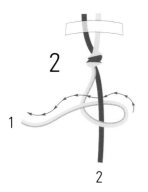

3. Now, repeat the process in order to make a double-knot. You've made your first complete left-loop knot!

Hint: After tying a RIGHT LOOP KNOT, string 1 will lay on the RIGHT side of string 2. After tying a LEFT LOOP KNOT string 2 will lay on the LEFT of string 1.

Simple Stripes

Now it is time to start knotting! This is the most straightforward, knotted bracelet to make, as it only requires one type of knot that is repeated over and over. Work slowly until you get the rhythm of the knotting and then it will be a breeze to finish!

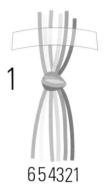

1. Choose six colors and cut a 28-inch/70-cm piece of each color. Tie a knot at the top and tape the knot to your work surface. (Tip: To make it easier to follow the instructions the first time, choose the same colors and order as those shown in the diagrams.)

654321

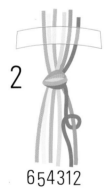

654312

2. You are going to start by making a LEFT LOOP KNOT (see page 22). Pick up your rightmost string, which will be string 1, and tie a LEFT LOOP KNOT over string 2.

3. Still using string 1, tie a LEFT LOOP KNOT over string 3.

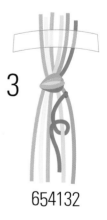

654132

4. Using string 1, tie a LEFT LOOP KNOT over string 4.

5. Using string 1, tie a LEFT LOOP KNOT over string 5.

6. Using string 1, tie a LEFT LOOP KNOT over string 6.

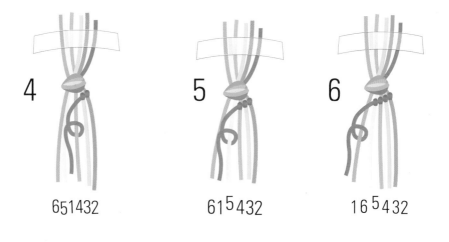

4

651432

5

61 5 432

6

16 5 432

Hint: Don't forget, to make one complete LEFT LOOP KNOT you will tie the thread TWO times. See pages 22-23 to remind yourself if you need to!

Swirls

After all that knotting, here is a fun bracelet to try that has a different look to it; a row of knot swirls down the bracelet! It is just as straightforward, and the knots twist themselves around the bracelet naturally, as you go. Again, be patient and knot carefully for neat results. You want the knots to move from one color to the next without any gaps.

48 in/120 cm 1 per color	20 in/50 cm 2 per color

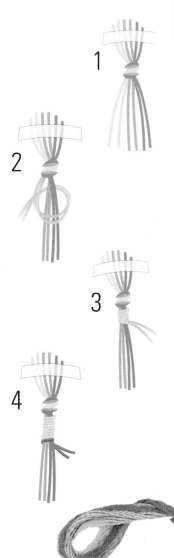

1. Choose three colors, and cut to the lengths shown in the chart. Knot your strings and secure.

2. Select a color to start with, holding the remaining strings in your hand in a bunch. Make a LEFT LOOP KNOT over all of the strings and pull it up tightly to the top of your bracelet.

3. Continue making LEFT LOOP KNOTS until you would like to switch colors. The knots will spiral around the bracelet as you are knotting. You will need to pass the string around the back of the bracelet after you have made about eight knots so that it continues to spiral properly.

4. When you wish to switch colors, select a thread that is closest to the knot that you just completed. When you make the next knot, it will sit close to the previous one and not leave a gap. Make sure you add the old color of strings to the group of strings you are knotting around.

5. When you have knotted your bracelet to the correct length, tie the strings in a knot at the bottom, and if you like, you can braid the ends.

The Criss Cross

This bracelet is a variation of the Simple Stripes bracelet on page 26. This time, you will use a LEFT LOOP KNOT and a RIGHT LOOP KNOT. You may find it easier to use the colors shown below the first time so you can match the steps exactly, and then select your own colors when you understand the pattern.

72 in/180 cm	36 in/90 cm
1 per color	2 per color

1. Cut your threads according to the chart measurements and knot them. Tie a knot at the top and tape the knot to your work surface.

2. Using the leftmost string (string 1), tie a RIGHT LOOP KNOT over each of string 2, string 3, string 4, string 5 and then string 6.

3. Repeat this step with the remaining five colors, always working from the left to the right.

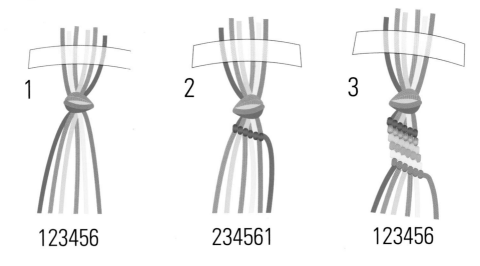

1   2   3

123456   234561   123456

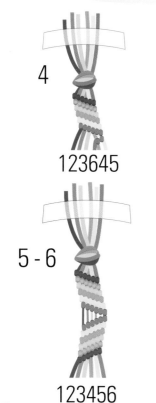

4

123645

5 - 6

123456

4. Now you are going to do the reverse of this to create the return pattern. Pick up string 6, which is back on the right side, and make a LEFT LOOP KNOT on string 5.

5. Carry on knotting string 6 with left loop knots on strings 4, 3, 2 and 1. It should now be on the left side of the bracelet.

6. Carry on with knotting, picking up the strings from the right and knotting back to the left until you have knotted all six colors.

7. Repeat steps 2 through 6, knotting left and then right with each of the strings until you are finished your bracelet. Tie it off and give it with pride!

Variation: Add a bead on the end strings each time you reverse the knotting. This creates a whole new look! Use beads that are large enough to thread, but not so large as to be awkward. Size E seed beads work well.

The Ladder

This bracelet is next in the book because it uses a combination of the wrapping and knotting techniques from the Swirls that you just made on page 31 and the straight knotting that you did to make Cupid's Arrow page 35. If you know how to make both of these bracelets, then even though this one looks quite tricky, you will find it a snap to make!

1

12345678

2-4

12345678

56 in/140 cm
1 per color

28 in/70 cm
2 per color

1. Cut four colors of threads. Knot them at the top and attach to your work surface.

2. Follow the instructions on page 33 for the Cupid's Arrow, knotting RIGHT LOOP KNOTS with String 1 from the left and then LEFT LOOP KNOTS from the right with String 8 to create a chevron. (Remember that "chevron" is the word used to describe a wide V shape.) Don't forget to knot strings 1 and 8 in the middle to make the point of the chevron.

3. Repeat this with each of the threads until you have created a chevron with each color.

4. Once you have knotted four chevrons, split the strings into two groups, making sure you have one of each color in each group.

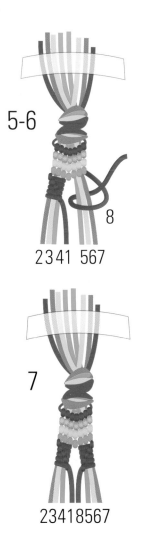

5-6

8

2 3 4 1   5 6 7

7

2 3 4 1 8 5 6 7

5. Now you are going to use the same instructions as you used to make the Swirl Bracelet on page 29. Choose one color of thread from the group on the left, and start to make LEFT LOOP KNOTS over the remaining three threads in that group of strings. Make ten knots with the left group of strings.

6. Now using the same color from the right group of strings, make ten RIGHT LOOP KNOTS over the remaining threads in that group of strings.

7. Now spread your strings back out in the same order as they are in the diagram.

8. Repeat steps 2 through 7 until you have the length of bracelet you wish, and then tie the threads in a knot to finish it.

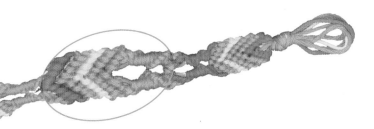

Hint: This is a great bracelet to add beads to. Slide the bead over the thread that you are using to knot the Swirl section of the pattern, right before you switch back to the Cupid's Arrow pattern. It looks really cool!

Patchwork Stripes

This funky bracelet uses exactly the same techniques as the Simple Stripes, but by changing the order of the strings that you knot over, you get a completely different look! This is a bright, colorful bracelet made from six strands, but you can experiment and see what it would look like with eight strands, or even try ten for a different effect.

The trick to this bracelet is to be able to work the strings in a forwards and backwards order. It is really quite simple to do and creates a great pattern. Try it with colors that are similar to each other to create a totally different look.

64 in/160 cm
1 per color

32 in/80 cm
2 per color

For a six-color, six-strand bracelet:

1. Select six colors and cut to the appropriate lengths.
Knot them at the top and tape them to your work surface.

2. Instead of starting with the end thread, we are going to start with the thread second from the right (string 5).
Pick up string 5 and make a RIGHT LOOP KNOT over string 6.
Look at the new order of the strings: string 5 and string 6 have now reversed positions.

3. Work backwards now by picking up string 4. Tie RIGHT LOOP KNOTS over string 6 and string 5.

1 2 3 4 5 6

2

1 2 3 4 6 5

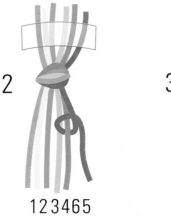

3

1 2 3 6 5 4

4. Now pick up string 3 and tie RIGHT LOOP KNOTS over strings 6, 5 and 4. Can you start to see the pattern? You are picking up the strings in a reverse order, but still knotting forward.

5. Pick up string 2 and tie RIGHT LOOP KNOTS over strings 6, 5, 4 and 3.

6. Pick up string 1 and tie RIGHT LOOP KNOTS over strings 6, 5, 4, 3 and 2.

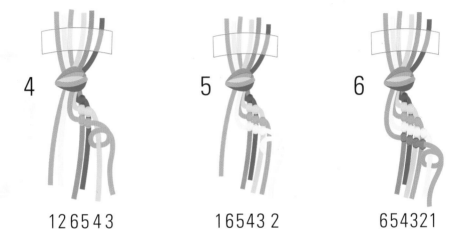

4
1 2 6 5 4 3

5
1 6 5 4 3 2

6
6 5 4 3 2 1

Now, look at the order of your threads, they have completely reversed! String 6 is now on the left, and string 1 is on the right. Guess what the next part of the pattern is?

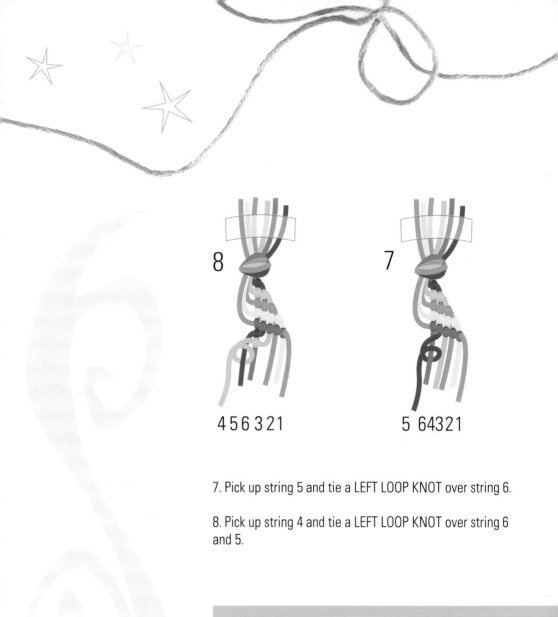

8

7

4 5 6 3 2 1

5 6 4 3 2 1

7. Pick up string 5 and tie a LEFT LOOP KNOT over string 6.

8. Pick up string 4 and tie a LEFT LOOP KNOT over string 6 and 5.

As you finish this bracelet, you will notice that you are now starting to use more of one color in a bracelet than others. So make sure you cut them long enough initially and trim the ends when you are done so they are even.

9. Pick up string 3 and tie LEFT LOOP KNOTS over strings 6, 5 and 4.

10. Pick up string 2 and tie LEFT LOOP KNOTS over strings 6, 5, 4 and 3.

11. Pick up string 1 and tie LEFT LOOP KNOTS over strings 6, 5, 4, 3 and 2.

9

3 4 5 6 2 1

10

2 3 4 5 6 1

11

1 2 3 4 5 6

You are now back to the beginning of the pattern. Start again at step 2, and repeat each step until you have tied a bracelet that is the correct length for you. Knot the threads at the end and tie on your wrist!

41

Diamond Weave

This is a more complicated bracelet to make, but with such a pretty pattern it is worth the time it takes to master it! Your friends will be thrilled to receive this bracelet, so go slowly and pay attention to the order of the forward and backward knots, as well as to your place in the pattern. You can do it!

🔵 20 in/50 cm   🔻 20 in/50 cm

1. The first thing to do is to lay out your strings in the proper order, as shown in the diagram. We suggest you use the same colors we do the first time so that you are able to learn the pattern more easily.

2. The first four rows of knots will be chevrons, as you did in Cupid's Arrow on page 33. Remember how this goes? Start with string 1 and tie RIGHT LOOP KNOTS over strings 2, 3 and 4.

3. Pick up string 8 and tie LEFT LOOP KNOTS over strings 7, 6 and 5.

4. Tie a RIGHT LOOP KNOT with strings 1 and 8 which are now in the center.

5. Go ahead and continue with strings 2 and 7, 3 and 6 and 4 and 5 until you have four chevrons.

6. Now you are going to tie the knots that create the red knot at the side of the large "X" shape.

1

12345678

2 - 6

12345678

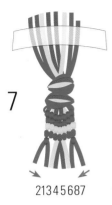

7

21345687

8 - 9

42136875

10 - 11

64218753

12 - 13

78645312

7. With strings 1 and 2, tie a RIGHT LOOP KNOT. Then with strings 7 and 8, tie a LEFT LOOP KNOT.

8. Next you are going to start knotting the bottom half of the "X", and the reverse chevrons. With string 4, LEFT LOOP KNOT over string 3, 1 and 2.

9. With string 5, RIGHT LOOP KNOT over string 6, 8 and 7.

10. With string 3, tie RIGHT LOOP KNOTS over strings 6, 8, 7 and 5.

11. With string 6, tie LEFT LOOP KNOTS over 1, 2 and 4.

12. With string 1, tie RIGHT LOOP KNOTS over string 8, 7, 5 and 6.

13. With string 8, tie LEFT LOOP KNOTS over string 2, 4, and 6. Then with string 2, tie RIGHT LOOP KNOTS over string 7, 5, and 3. Continue to knot the two sets of red strings until you see a mirror image of the top half.

Southern Trinidad

This adapted V pattern looks easier than the Diamond Weave, but don't be deceived! If you master the Diamond Weave pattern first, this one will be a snap. On this bracelet you will see that you knot the middle strings first, and then the outer edges. Then you move back to the middle strings. So you aren't working in a row the way you have previously. The results look great though, and the colors are pretty: it's one of our favorite bracelets in the book! Be patient and have fun making the Southern Trinidad.

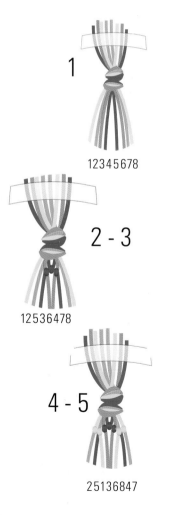

64 in/160 cm
1 per color

32 in/80 cm
2 per color

1. Cut and knot your strings, lay them out in the same color order as we do.

2. Start with the center "v" by picking up string 4 and tying a RIGHT LOOP KNOT over string 5, and then another RIGHT LOOP KNOT string 6.

3. With string 5, tie a LEFT LOOP KNOT over string 3.

4. Now you are moving to the left edge and must use string 1 to tie a RIGHT LOOP KNOT over string 2, and then again over 5.

5. Now to the right edge and use string 8 to tie a LEFT LOOP KNOT over string 7, followed by one over 4.

Check your string order, it should be 25136847.

6 - 7

25618347

3 - 11

56218734

6. Now back to the center. String 3 RIGHT LOOP KNOTS over each of string 6 and 8.

7. Use string 6 to tie a LEFT LOOP KNOT over string 1.

8. Back to the left side. String 2 RIGHT LOOP KNOTS over 5 and 6.

9. On the right side, string 7 LEFT LOOP KNOTS over string 4 and 3 (56218734). Again, check your string order to help you stay on track.

10. In the center, use string 1 to make RIGHT LOOP KNOTS over string 8 and 7.

11. Use string 8 to make a LEFT LOOP KNOTS over string 2.

12 - 13

68527413

14 - 17

87654321

12. On the left, string 5 RIGHT LOOP KNOTS over string 6 and string 8.

13. On the right, string 4 LEFT LOOP KNOTS over strings 3 and 1.

14. Back the center use string 2 to tie RIGHT LOOP KNOTS over strings 7 and 4.

15. Use string 7 to tie a LEFT LOOP KNOT over string 5.

16. On the left, string 6 RIGHT LOOP KNOTS over strings 8 and 7.

17. On the right, string 3 LEFT LOOP KNOTS over strings 1 and 2 (87654321). Check your ending string order to make sure you are on track.

You have just completed the entire pattern! Did you notice that your strings have ended up in the reverse order of how you started? Because this bracelet has two of each color, you won't see a difference when you repeat the pattern. If you used six different colors though, when you repeat the pattern, the order of the colors will be reversed.

Why don't you try six colors with your next bracelet to see how pretty the results are?

Trinidad

Up until now, all of the knotted, flat bracelets were made by placing a knot on every string in every row. With the Trinidad bracelet however, we start using the technique of skipping knots. This creates the almost "lacey" effect in the bracelet and is very elegant. Use two colors that are quite different from each other the first time so that you can see what you are doing more clearly.

1

12345678

60 in/150 cm
2 per color

30 in/75 cm
4 per color

1. Cut your strings, knot them at the top and tape the knot to your work surface. Arrange your threads as shown, with four strands of one color in the middle, and two strands each of the second color on each side.

2. Start by working on the edges. Use string 1 and make a RIGHT LOOP KNOT over string 2 and string 3.

3. Use string 8 to make a LEFT LOOP KNOT over string 7 and 6.

4. Now use string 3 to make a RIGHT LOOP KNOT over string 1 and 4.

5. Use string 6 to make a LEFT LOOP KNOT over string 8 and 5. (21436587)

6. Use string 3 to make a RIGHT LOOP KNOT over string 6 to complete the chevron.

2 - 3

23145867

4 - 6

21463587

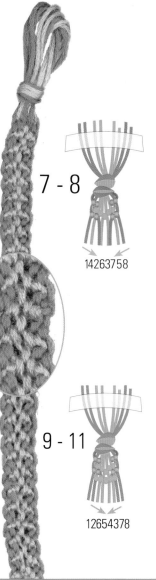

7 - 8

14263758

9 - 11

12654378

7. Now look at the diagram and see how the knots are positioned. Strings 2 and 7 are on the outside edges, and weren't used to make knots on your last row. Now use string 2 to make a RIGHT LOOP KNOT over strings 1 and 4. Do you see how you skipped past the knots you worked in your last row to start a new row? This is what will make the scallop edge of your bracelet.

8. Use string 7 to make a LEFT LOOP KNOT over strings 8 and 5.

9. Move to the inside and pick up string 4 and make RIGHT LOOP KNOTS over strings 2 and 6. (12643758)

10. Use string 5 to make LEFT LOOP KNOTS over strings 7 and 3 (12645378).

11. Now use string 4 to make a RIGHT LOOP KNOT over string 5.

Repeat the pattern from step 2 to 11 until your bracelet is long enough and tie off with a knot.

Hint: Tension refers to how tightly or how loosely the threads are knotted. Until now, it hasn't been terribly important. With this bracelet, however, you will want to pay attention to this, and try to keep the knots consistent — not too tight, not too loose, in order to create an even pattern. Try this bracelet using four different colors — two strands of each and see what the effect is.

Super Stripes

The Super Stripes bracelet is a lot like the very first one you did, Simple Stripes, in that all of the knots move in one direction only. So choose which direction you would like to knot in. We chose to do LEFT LOOP KNOTS for this bracelet, but it would work just as well with RIGHT LOOP KNOTS.

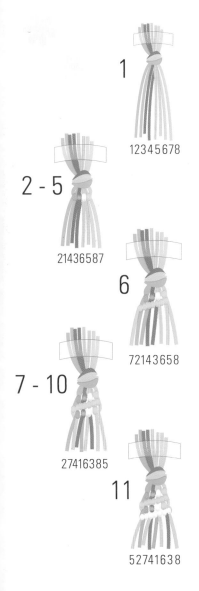

1

12345678

2 - 5

21436587

6

72143658

7 - 10

27416385

11

52741638

60 in/150 cm	32 in/80 cm
1 per color	2 per color

1. Cut and knot your threads. Arrange the thread colors in pairs.

2. With 7 and 8, tie a LEFT LOOP KNOT.

3. With strings 5 and 6, tie a LEFT LOOP KNOT.

4. With strings 3 and 4, tie a LEFT LOOP KNOT.

5. With strings 1 and 2, tie a LEFT LOOP KNOT.

6. Now, start with string 7, and the right end, and tie LEFT LOOP KNOTS all the way across — on strings 8, 5, 6, 3, 4, 1 and 2.

7. With string 8, tie a LEFT LOOP KNOT over string 5.

8. With string 6, tie a LEFT LOOP KNOT over string 3.

9. With string 4, tie a LEFT LOOP KNOT over string 1.

10. With string 2, tie a LEFT LOOP KNOT over string 7.

11. Now go back to the right side and use string 5 to tie a LEFT LOOP KNOT over string 8, 3, 6, 1, 4, 7 and 2.

How easy is this? I'll bet you thought it would be tough, but we threw an easy one in here because we thought you would like a break from the tough bracelets. Good job, and have fun repeating this pattern until your bracelet is finished. Happy knotting!

Eternity Bracelet

This is such a great bracelet! It looks fantastic on, and is a wonderful gift to give and receive. It is one of the more time-consuming bracelets in the book, but with the skills you have gained up to this point, you should be able to master this one before too long. You will work this one almost as two separate bracelets, only meeting in the middle to connect and cross over. Although there are a lot of steps, don't worry; it is just because you have to work each side separately. You repeat the same pattern, though, so it is quite simple really.

	68 in/175 cm 1 per color		34 in/85 cm 2 per color

1

12345678

1. Cut, knot and tape your threads to your work surface. Arrange the thread colors in pairs.

2. You are going to start knotting chevrons, but you are not going to tie the center knot. This keeps the two parts of the bracelet separate. So start with string 1 and tie RIGHT LOOP KNOTS over strings 2, 3 and 4.

3. With string 8, tie LEFT LOOP KNOTS over strings 7, 6 and 5.

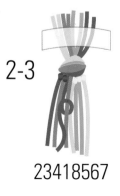

2-3

23418567

4 - 9

12345678

10

12354678

11

51236784

4. With string 2 tie RIGHT LOOP KNOTS over strings 3, 4 and 1.

5. With string 7, tie LEFT LOOP KNOTS over strings 6, 5 and 8.

6. With string 3, tie RIGHT LOOP KNOT over strings 4, 1 and 2.

7. With string 6, tie LEFT LOOP KNOTS over strings 5, 8 and 7.

8. With string 4, tie RIGHT LOOP KNOTS over strings 1, 2 and 3.

9. With String 5, tie LEFT LOOP KNOTS over strings 8, 7 and 6. Your string order is now as it was in the beginning: 1, 2, 3, 4,5, 6 ,7 ,8.

10. You have half the loop done, and now you are going to join them together in the middle and cross over. Take string 4 and tie a RIGHT LOOP KNOT over string 5.

11. Then continue with string 4 knotting over strings 6, 7, and 8. Take string 5 and LEFT LOOP KNOT over 3, 2, and 1.

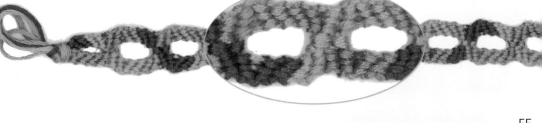

12 - 13

65127843

12. Now reverse the chevron pattern for two rows. With string 3, RIGHT LOOP KNOT over strings 6, 7, 8, and 4. (51236784)

13. With string 6, LEFT LOOP KNOT over string 2, 1 and 5.

14. Now start the half chevron pattern again, but this time with your colors on the opposite sides of your bracelet. With string 6, RIGHT LOOP KNOT over strings 5, 1 and 2.

15. With string 3, LEFT LOOP KNOT over string 4, 8 and 7.

16. With string 5, RIGHT LOOP KNOT over string 1, 2 and 6.

17. With string 4, LEFT LOOP KNOT over string 8, 7 and 3.

18. With string 1, RIGHT LOOP KNOT over string 2, 6 and 5.

14 - 17

12654378

19. With string 8, LEFT LOOP KNOT over string 7, 3 and 4.

20. With string 2, RIGHT LOOP KNOT over string 6, 5 and 1.

21. With string 7, LEFT LOOP KNOT over string 3, 4 and 8.

22. Now refer back to step 10 and continue to knot your eternity bracelet, by joining the two sides in the center.

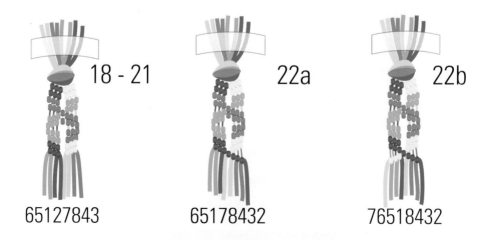

18 - 21

65127843

22a

65178432

22b

76518432

To Finish: You have now completed the separate sides and you are going to join the loop again. So start with step 10 and follow the pattern through to the end. Repeat steps 10 to 22 until you have a bracelet long enough to wear.

The Zipper

We decided to put this bracelet in the book as a final challenge. It looks deceptively easy, but uses an entirely different style of knotting to create the zipper tooth effect. To make your first bracelet, we recommend using two colors that contrast in order to see how it is going along as you knot. Pay attention to the "**overs**" and "**unders**" in order to get the right effect, as well as to the tension so that the pattern remains even.

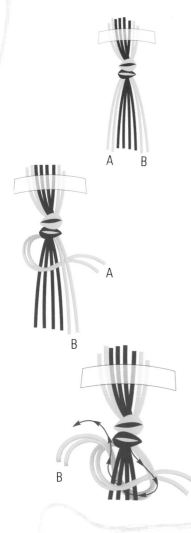

1. Choose two colors of threads and cut four pieces of each — about 12 inches/ 30cm long for the center color, and 24 inches/ 60 cm long for the outer colors. Knot the strings and tape them to your work surface.

2. Arrange the shorter threads in the center and two of the longer threads on each side. Pick up the two strands on the left (A) and cross them **over** the strings in the center leaving a bit of a loop on the left and pass it **under** strands B (almost like the shape of a "4").

3. Now pick up strands B and pass them **under** strands A and the center strands, and pull them **up** through the loop on the left side. Pull the knot tight, sliding it up to the top.

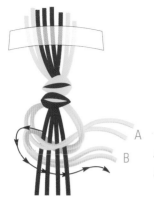

4. Strands A and B have now switched sides. Take strands B, and pass them **under** the center strands and **over** strands A.

5. Take strands A and pass them **over** the center strands and **down** through the loop and pull the knot tight, sliding it to the top.

That is it! It seems easy, but requires you to pay attention to the directions. Keep knotting until your bracelet is finished, and then tie it off.

Record Log

We hope that you continue to enjoy creating friendship bracelets and giving them to people you care about. They are a wonderful way to tell your friends that you think they are special and that they are worth the work it took to make these beautiful tokens!

These final few pages are a place where you can keep track of the bracelets you create and who you give them to.

Bracelet _____

Made By _____

Given To _____

Date _____

Notes _____

_____

_____

Bracelet _____

Made By _____

Given To _____

Date _____

Notes _____

_____

_____

Bracelet _____

Made By _____

Given To _____

Date _____

Notes _____

_____

_____

Bracelet _____

Made By _____

Given To _____

Date _____

Notes _____

_____

_____

Bracelet _____

Made By _____

Given To _____

Date _____

Notes _____

_____

_____

inches

0

1

2

3

4

5

6

cm
0
1
2
3
4
5
6
7
8
9
10
11
12
13
14
15
16
17

Bracelet _____
Made By _____
Given To _____
Date _____
Notes _____
_____
_____

Bracelet _____
Made By _____
Given To _____
Date _____
Notes _____
_____
_____

Bracelet _____
Made By _____
Given To _____
Date _____
Notes _____
_____
_____

Bracelet _____

Made By _____

Given To _____

Date _____

Notes _____

_____

_____

Bracelet _____

Made By _____

Given To _____

Date _____

Notes _____

_____

_____

Bracelet _____

Made By _____

Given To _____

Date _____

Notes _____

_____

_____

inches

0

1

2

3

4

5

6